THE U.S. MARINE CORPS

THE U.S. MARINE CORPS

J.F. Warner

 Lerner Publications Company • Minneapolis

For Peggy, who taught me how to live

The author is especially grateful to the following Marines who so graciously gave of their time and effort in researching the answers to a myriad of questions and in helping assure the accuracy of facts: Major Doug Erly of the public affairs office in Boston, Massachusetts; Captain Mike O'Donnell of the Marine Detachment at the Naval Education and Training Center in Newport, Rhode Island; Chief Warrant Officer Randy Gaddo of the public affairs office at Marine Corps Headquarters in Washington, D. C.; Staff Sergeant Greg Maslen of the recruiting office in Middletown, Rhode Island; and Sergeant William Bennett of the recruiting office in Boston, Massachusetts.

Copyright © 1991 by J. F. Warner
Second printing 1993 includes updated information.

Library of Congress Cataloging-in-Publication Data

Warner, J. F.
    The U.S. Marine Corps / J.F. Warner.
        p.   cm.
    Includes index.
    Summary: Reviews the history, modern day life, and equipment of the Marine Corps, and details the enlistment and promotion procedures.
    ISBN 0-8225-1432-X
    1. United States. Marine Corps—Juvenile literature. [1. United States. Marine Corps.] I. Title.
VE23.W37   1991
359.9'6'0973—dc20   90-19327
                                                                CIP
                                                                AC

Manufactured in the United States of America

2   3   4   5   6   96   95   94   93

CONTENTS

Introduction . . . 7

1
The Corps Is Born . . . 11

2
The Corps Comes of Age . . . 25

3
The Once and Future Corps . . . 41

4
Joining the Marines . . . 51

5
Life after Boot Camp . . . 63

6
Going for the Gold . . . 73

Conclusion . . . 84

Appendix . . . 85

Index . . . 86

Combat-ready Marines charge out of an amphibious assault vehicle during a training exercise.

Introduction

Corporal Lester Barney stole a look at his watch. It read 0515—5:15 A.M. Overhead the first signs of dawn were forming in a cloudless blue sky. This promised to be another warm, inviting June day.

But Corporal Barney could not see any of this. For the last half hour he had been crouched in an AAV with the other riflemen in his infantry squad. The AAV, or amphibious assault vehicle, was one of several poised on the lower deck of a Navy tank landing ship.

Each AAV held 25 Marines in full battle dress. Corporal Barney had already checked his four-man team and its gear for the last time. As he expected, they were ready.

No one spoke. Had anyone tried, his words would have been drowned out by the roar of the AAV's powerful diesel engines. At 0530 hours, the giant stern of the tank landing ship was lowered to form a ramp. Then, one by one, like great lumbering beasts, the AAVs rolled down the ramp and into the sea.

In minutes they formed a line with other assault vehicles from other ships in the assembled fleet. On signal they headed toward the beach, a little more than a mile away.

As the AAVs moved ashore, Harrier jets made one final bomb run across the landing zone. Overhead a squadron of Sea Stallion helicopters was rushing other Marine infantry to the beach.

By then, the fleet's big guns had already stopped firing.

Navy frogmen had already cleared the landing zone of any mines or underwater obstacles. On this day, the Marines were practicing what they have become noted for the world over. This was an amphibious assault on an "enemy-held" shore.

Corporal Barney had lost track of the number of practice landings he had been part of. In his four years in the Marine Corps it had to be at least a dozen, he thought. There were three in the Mediterranean a few months ago, and two more on islands in the Caribbean. There were at least six or seven here at Onslow Beach in North Carolina. If he stayed in the Corps for 20 or 30 years, he would end up being in many more.

But should he stay? Should he become a career Marine? That was a question Les Barney had been wrestling with for weeks. He had enlisted right out of high school. He'd thought

An amphibious assault vehicle approaches Onslow Beach on the coast of North Carolina. Onslow Beach is the site of numerous Marine Corps training exercises.

While the Marine Corps is made up of many people with specialized jobs, infantry is the heart of the Corps, and all Marines are expected to learn how to handle a rifle.

about college, but didn't feel he was ready at the time. Besides, getting the money together would have been a problem.

To tell the truth, Les hadn't quite known what he wanted to do after high school. He wasn't sure he knew enough about himself to make a good choice. That's when he turned to the Marines.

He enlisted for four years. His test scores were strong enough that he could have had his pick of career fields. But he chose infantry. After all, Les thought, the infantry *is* the Corps. Even his recruiting sergeant had told him that every Marine, no matter what job he worked at, was a rifleman first.

Boot camp went well. In fact, Les won a special promotion to private first class there. Then he was off to SOI, the School of Infantry, for eight weeks.

At SOI Les heard of a call for volunteers to serve two years in London, England. He applied and was accepted. Les was promoted to lance corporal in England.

Then he was assigned to the FMF, the Fleet Marine Force, back in the United States. He joined the Second Marine Division at Camp Lejeune, North Carolina, and was put into an infantry platoon. Four months later, he was promoted to corporal. Now his pay was more than $1,000 a month. More important, he was placed in charge of other Marines. He was learning to be a leader.

With the money he had saved, and some the government added, Les had enough now to pay for at least two years of college. But if he reenlisted, he would get a bonus of several thousand dollars. And he knew he could take college courses in the Corps. If he was good enough, they'd even pay him to go to college full time.

Besides, Les liked being a Marine. He had made some good friends in the Corps. He liked the feeling of *esprit de corps*, the common enthusiasm and togetherness among the group, that came with being a Marine. He was learning that he could handle responsibilities. He was confident without being cocky.

He had already seen more of the world than he ever imagined he would. There was also so much more waiting to be seen. Perhaps he would sign up for another hitch. After all, Les thought, he was only 21. A whole lifetime lay ahead of him.

1
The Corps Is Born

The United States Marine Corps was born on November 10, 1775. That was just seven months after the battles of Lexington and Concord opened the American Revolution. It would be eight more months before the Declaration of Independence was adopted.

The Second Continental Congress, meeting in Philadelphia, voted to raise two battalions of Marines, about 1,000

Samuel Nicholas, leader of the Continental Marines

men in all. They were to be "inlisted and commissioned to serve for and during the present war between Great Britain and the colonies." What is more, those "inlisted" had to be experienced sailors, or at least familiar with maritime life, so they could serve "to advantage by sea, when required."

These would not be the first Marines the world saw, however. The British themselves had maintained a marine corps for 100 years. What is more, the idea of seagoing soldiers, which is what the Marines really are, goes back some 5,000 years, to the world of the Phoenicians, Egyptians, and early Greeks. So it was no surprise when the Second Continental Congress called for a marine corps in the war against Britain.

The first 100 recruits, all volunteers, arrived in Philadelphia on December 5, 1775. To lead them, Congress named a 32-year-old Quaker, Samuel B. Nicholas, as captain. He was the first officer in the Continental Marines.

A well-equipped unit of Continental Marines charges into battle during the Revolutionary War.

Marines aboard the *Bonhomme Richard* were instrumental in the crew's capture of the British warship *Serapis.*

Off to War

Just four months later, on Sunday, March 3, 1776, the Continental Marines went to war. A small force led by Captain Nicholas rowed ashore from ships anchored off New Providence Island in the Bahamas. In short order, the Marines captured two forts, three ships, and some gunpowder, shot, and cannons. They also took several prisoners. One of these was the British governor of the Bahama Islands.

As battles go, this was not an especially important one. Yet it was the first amphibious landing the Marines ever made. Above all, the U.S. Marines have become known the world over as the experts in amphibious warfare.

13

On to Victory

As the Revolutionary War unfolded, Marines were found in the thick of battle. On land they fought alongside soldiers led by Colonel Benedict Arnold in the North. They were part of General George Washington's army in the East. They clashed with British troops in the southern colonies and in lands as far west as what is now Illinois.

At sea, Marines could be found on every ship in the Continental Navy. The seagoing Marines had their shining moment aboard the *Bonhomme Richard* with Captain John Paul Jones, the "Father of the United States Navy." Marines aboard ship turned the tide of battle in Jones's epic sea fight with the British warship *Serapis* off the coast of England in September of 1779.

Finally, Marines were there when the British surrendered at Yorktown, Virginia, on October 19, 1781. The Revolutionary War was over, and the new country—along with its Marines—was eager to take its place in the world.

The Corps Disbands

Before that happened, however, Congress decided the United States didn't need any armed forces. Less than two years after the end of the American Revolution, the last Continental Marine was sent home.

For the next several years, the United States did not have an active army or navy. The country's leaders learned, though, that not having a military made the United States an easy target for the bullies of the world. In short order, France, Barbary pirates, and Great Britain itself tried to take advantage of the defenseless new country.

Battling the Bullies

Shortly after Congress disbanded the Army and Navy, French warships began seizing U.S. merchant sailors at sea. Next, French warships were raiding vessels that were docked in U.S. ports.

At the same time, the British were doing the same thing. They claimed the sailors they took off U.S. ships were really British citizens.

With these attacks on private ships, Congress realized it had made a mistake in disbanding the Army and Navy. It ordered the building of a half dozen ships and enlisted Marines and sailors to serve on them. By 1797, three of the new warships had been launched. One of these was the famous USS *Constitution*, or "Old Ironsides," as it came to be called.

The modern Marine Corps was created shortly after Marines were enlisted to serve on the USS *Constitution*, shown here in battle against Britain's *Guerriere* during the War of 1812.

The following year Congress passed an act "establishing and organizing a Marine Corps." That act created the Marine Corps as it is known in modern times.

While the French and British were pillaging U.S. ships close to home, another kind of outrage was taking place across the Atlantic Ocean. Pirates from the Barbary states in northern Africa began raiding U.S. merchant ships. At first Congress reacted shamefully. It paid nearly two million dollars in tributes and ransom to the pirates. The money was supposed to stop the raids. It did not.

By 1805, people in the United States were fed up. A force of Marines, led by Lieutenant Presley O'Bannon, was sent to unseat the pasha—or ruler—of Tripoli, the Barbary state that raided the most U.S. ships. O'Bannon and his Marines defeated the pasha, who was replaced on the throne by his brother, Hamet, a U.S. ally. To express thanks, Hamet presented O'Bannon with a sword. Copies of that sword are still carried by Marine officers.

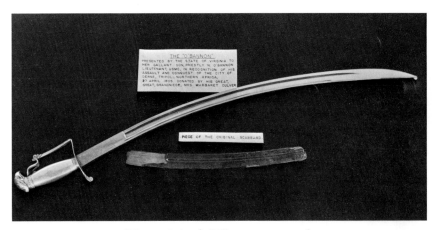

The original O'Bannon sword

"Old Ironsides" and the Marines serving aboard it were crucial to the U.S. military's strength during the country's early years.

Once the United States had stopped most of the Barbary pirates and the French from raiding its ships, it turned its attention to the British. On June 18, 1812, the United States declared war.

When the war began, there were 42 officers and 1,523 men in the Marine Corps. The first Marines to fight were the 51 aboard the USS *Constitution* when it met the British warship *Guerriere* in August. Other sea battles followed, several including Marines aboard Old Ironsides. Marines also fought brilliantly in battles on Lake Erie and Lake Champlain, and on other ships in the faraway Pacific Ocean.

On land, the Marines could be found anywhere a battle was brewing. They fought valiantly while trying to save the capital city of Washington from the invading British. Marines also played an important role in the biggest fight of the war. In the Battle of New Orleans, Marines helped General Andrew Jackson defeat the British. For their heroic efforts, Congress passed a resolution. It read, in part: "Resolved, That Congress entertain a high sense of the valour and conduct of...Marines...in the defence of the city."

Once again, the United States was at peace. And once again, the very existence of the Marine Corps was threatened. Its force was reduced to fewer than 1,000 officers and enlisted men. By 1830, the U.S. Army wanted to abolish the Corps. Andrew Jackson, by then president, wanted the Army to take it over. As the arguments raged on, more than a few people recalled a story that had its beginnings after the Revolutionary War.

When the armed forces were disbanded in the 1780s, the story went, all that was left was an outfit of mules and two battalions of Marines. The Army and the Navy tossed a coin to see who would take the Marines and who would take the mules. The Army won the coin toss. It chose the mules!

Fortunately for the Marines, Congress stepped in this time. It passed a second act on June 30, 1834. This one made clear that the Marines were responsible only to the Navy. The act also set the strength of the Corps at 1,287 officers and enlisted men.

Finally, the 1834 act gave the rank of colonel to the Marines' commandant. After the Civil War, which ended in 1865, the commandant's rank was raised to brigadier general. In the years that followed, the commandant's rank continued to rise—to major general, lieutenant general, and finally to full, or four-star, general, where it remains.

Colonel Archibald Henderson served as commandant of the Marine Corps for nearly 40 years.

The Henderson Years

October 18, 1820, was an important day in the history of the Marine Corps. That was the day Archibald Henderson became its fifth commandant. He was to stay on the job 38 years, until his death in 1859.

The years Colonel Henderson served as commandant were years in which the United States extended its borders and influence both at home and around the world. In 1820, there were fewer than nine million people living in 22 states. The young nation stretched only as far west as Illinois. By 1860, the year following Henderson's death, nearly 30 million people were living in 32 states. By then, the country's borders had extended to the Pacific Ocean and included the states of California and Oregon.

The Battle of Chapultepec during the Mexican War allowed the Marines to occupy the national palace, which became known as the halls of Montezuma, in Mexico City.

Under Commandant Henderson, Marines steadily gained a wider role in the affairs of the country. Hardly a place in the world—from remote islands in the Pacific Ocean to the Philippines and even China—had not been visited by U.S. Marines.

Closer to home, Marines took an active part in the war with Mexico (1846-1848). The war settled the border dispute between Texas and Mexico. Mexico was also forced to give up huge areas of land in what is now California, Nevada, New Mexico, Utah, and Arizona.

Among the battles Marines fought in this war, one stands out. The Battle of Chapultepec, on a hill overlooking Mexico City, was the most memorable in the history of the Corps to that time. Taking the fortress on the hill was the key to

20

winning Mexico City—and the war. In a brief but savage fight, Marines took the hill and the city. Not long after, a red stripe was added to the dress blue trousers Marines wear. The stripe is said to be a symbol for the Marines who fell at Chapultepec.

In the years following the war with Mexico, the Marines remained quite active. The United States continued its expansionist policies, and Marines were there at every step.

Chief among these adventures was an expedition to Japan. In 1853, Commodore Matthew Calbraith Perry, accompanied by 200 Marines, boldly sailed into Tokyo Bay.

Commodore Perry succeeded in landing in Tokyo Bay because he impressed the Japanese with his show of military force. Other U.S. ships had tried to land there, but had always been fired upon. With his ship's crew prepared to engage in battle and backed by Marines, Perry managed to present President Fillmore's letter to high-ranking representatives of the emperor.

The commodore wished to present a letter from President Millard Fillmore to the highest Japanese official he could find. The Japanese demanded that the Americans leave. Perry refused. Thanks in part to the 200 Marines at his side, he finally won his case. The Japanese accepted the letter, which spelled out terms of a treaty that would allow the United States to have trading rights in Japan.

A year later, Commodore Perry and his Marines returned. This time, Perry arranged a treaty between the countries. After centuries of isolation, Japan was finally drawn into the mainstream of world affairs. Perhaps more than any other, this adventure strengthened the reputation of the Marines as the armed spearhead of the United States.

A Nation Divided

For the most part, expansion had opened up new lands for the United States. The population increased, and so did the country's wealth. The world began to take notice of this new nation, which was bursting with energy and high hopes.

But expansion brought problems, too. Not the least of these was the question of slavery. Arguments for and against slavery grew hotter with every new state taken into the Union. Finally, the conflict erupted with the Civil War in 1861.

This was one war in which the Marines did not make a difference. Many of its officers chose to leave the Union. Nearly all of these officers joined the Confederate Marines. Those who remained loyal to the federal government were given no clear role in the war. As a result, units were broken into small groups. A few Marines fought as part of Army units. Others operated guns on Navy warships.

The explosion that destroyed the USS *Maine* started the Spanish-American War. Even though no proof was found, U.S. officials strongly suspected that the blast came from a Spanish mine.

When the war ended in 1865, the Marine Corps again fell out of favor. The old effort to do away with the Marines began again. For the next 33 years, the Corps spent as much energy fighting for its existence as it did watching out for the interests of the United States at home and abroad.

War with Spain

All the efforts to abolish the Marines ended when the USS *Maine* blew up in the harbor of Havana, Cuba, on February 15, 1898. The explosion set off a swift, lopsided war with Spain that lasted four months. When it was over, Cuba was freed from Spanish rule. Puerto Rico, Guam, and the Philippine Islands were taken over by the United States. That same year, the United States claimed the Hawaiian Islands.

Little more than 100 years old, the United States was thrust fully into the spotlight as a world power. Marines had played a major role. From Yorktown to Yokohama, from Mexico to Manila, wherever the United States went, Marines were in the front ranks. Time and time again, the country had called on its Marines. Not once had they failed.

The Marine Corps used posters, such as this one by Sidney H. Reisenberg, to recruit Marines during World War I.

2
The Corps
Comes of Age

By the start of the 20th century, the Marines had already fought hundreds of battles. But none of these involved large numbers of troops.

Perhaps no more than 1,000 Marines took part in the entire American Revolution. The wars with Mexico and with Spain saw no more than 2,000 in the thick of things. Even Presley O'Bannon had only 18 Marines with him at Tripoli!

All this changed when the United States declared war on Germany in 1917. The declaration brought the United States into World War I.

By then, the war had been raging in Europe for more than three years. Millions of soldiers on both sides had died. Tens of millions more had been wounded. The Allies, led by England and France, were exhausted. The German army was planning one final push across France to end the war. Then came the U.S. forces, including the Marines. Before the war ended in victory for the Allies in 1918, nearly 32,000 U.S. Marines had seen battle.

War in France

Most people, including the Marines, thought the Corps would spend its time helping the Navy during the war. One person who did not, however, was the commandant. Major

Major General George Barnett was the 12th commandant of the Marine Corps, serving from 1914 to 1920.

General George Barnett insisted his Marines get into the fight. "I do not want the Marine Corps to be considered a police force," he argued. The Army objected, but the commandant had his way. A Marine brigade was attached to the Army.

The battle that earned the Marines their greatest honors in World War I was fought in Belleau Wood, a forest fewer than 50 miles from Paris—the capital city of France. If the Germans broke through Belleau Wood, they would seize Paris, and the war would be over. Germany would win.

Early in June 1918, the Marines entered Belleau Wood.

The French soldiers, exhausted from holding off the German attack, withdrew. As they left, a French officer told the U.S. Marines they would be wise to leave, too. The Marines' answer was swift and to the point. "Retreat?" one officer replied. "We just got here."

Again and again the Germans tried to drive the Marines out of the forest. Again and again they were turned back. Finally, after a month of savage fighting, the Germans themselves were driven out of Belleau Wood. Paris was saved.

The French government declared a national holiday. There was a huge parade in Paris to honor the U.S. forces. General John J. Pershing, commander of all U.S. forces in France, praised the Marines. "You stood like a wall against the enemy advance on Paris," he told them. The French general added his thanks. From that time on, he said, Belleau Wood was to

Marines operate a signal station in Belleau Wood during World War I.

The first women to join the Marine Corps enlisted during World War I.

be known as *Bois de la Brigade de Marine*—"Forest of the Marine Brigade." Even the Germans added their praise. Stunned by the reckless bravery of the Marines, they pinned a name on them. *Teufelhunde*—"Devil Dogs"—they called them.

Spurred by success at Belleau Wood, the United States went on the attack. In a series of battles over the next five months, the U.S. ground forces steadily drove the Germans back. Finally, the Germans had suffered enough. On November 11, 1918, they gave up. The long and terrible war was over.

Besides its battle honors, the Marine Corps saw two other important events during the war. One was the birth of its aviation arm. The second was the arrival of women into the Corps. About 300 women enlisted under the slogan "Free a Marine to Fight."

The Other Marines

During World War I, the Marine brigade in France received the headlines and the glory. But that was not the only job Marines were doing. In fact, 47,000 other Marines were scattered from Cuba to China, from the U.S. Virgin Islands to Russia. They proved once again that Marines serve wherever their president sends them. They do whatever is asked of them. As Marines say, "Marines are given orders and they go."

Two places the Marines were sent were the Caribbean and Central America. America's presence in these Central American and island nations began in earnest during the war with Spain in 1898. The Corps would remain there for 30 years. Marines were sent to Panama, Cuba, Nicaragua,

In the early 1900s, the Marine Corps was called on to help squash rebellions, stabilize the governments, and protect U.S. citizens in a number of other countries. Among the places to which Marines were deployed were Cuba, *above*, and China, *below*.

Honduras, Haiti, and the Dominican Republic. Their job was to keep foreign nations out of the Caribbean and Central America. The United States government wished to control those areas.

During these years, the largest number of Marines serving outside the United States could be found in China. As many as 5,000 of them stayed until November 1941, a month before the two countries joined the Allied forces in World War II. It was in China that Marines got the name "leatherneck," because of the high leather collar worn with the uniform.

Looking Ahead

While the Marine Corps was kept busy serving U.S. interests abroad, its top leaders were looking ahead. The Marines had won great honors in France during World War I. But Marines had served only as foot soldiers, as part of the Army. If this was to be its only role, why have a Marine Corps?

Addressing the question, the top Marine generals agreed the Corps's survival lay in amphibious warfare. Once that idea was accepted, the Marines set out to develop the best ways of landing troops from Navy ships onto enemy-held shores.

When the United States went to war again in 1941, U.S. Marines knew what their role would be. And they knew how to do it well. After all, they had been hard at work perfecting amphibious warfare for 20 years.

The War Begins

The Japanese attacked U.S. military bases in Hawaii on December 7, 1941. When that happened, World War II was

While a battleship burns nearby, rescuers pull survivors from the water at Pearl Harbor. The Japanese attack on the naval base in Hawaii forced the United States to join World War II.

already two years old. Germany had once again overrun most of Europe and North Africa. It was about to invade the Soviet Union. Alone, England was fighting for its life. Now the United States would join the fight against Germany, Italy, and Japan.

The Marines, military leaders decided, would confine their efforts to the Pacific. The Army would do the fighting in

Europe, and other Army troops would fight in the Pacific with the Marines. But this time, the war in the Pacific clearly belonged to the Marines.

Caught off guard by the Japanese attack, U.S. forces in the Pacific were hurt badly. In quick order, the Japanese over- whelmed Marines in China and on the island of Guam. Wake Island and the Philippines followed. The outlook was bleak. Then came the Battle of Midway.

On the Attack

Though it involved Marines on ships and on Midway Is- land in the Pacific, the battle really belonged to the Navy. In two days in June 1942, the U.S. Navy soundly defeated the Japanese. It sank four aircraft carriers and shot down more than 300 Japanese planes. When the planes went down, the core of the Japanese pilot force was lost. Japan's navy never recovered.

After Midway, U.S. leaders changed their plans. They sent the Marines on the attack. A series of amphibious landings on Japanese-held islands was planned. Each successful as- sault would bring the Marines that much closer to Japan. When they gained control of an island, U.S. forces could establish a base for the Navy and the Marines to rest, re- train, and refit. The first landing would be on the island of Guadalcanal.

The battle lasted six months. It was the longest for the Marines in World War II. It also stopped the Japanese ad- vance in its tracks. Of equal importance, it made veterans of those who took part. Now these battle-hardened Marines could train others in the ways of island war.

Leapfrogging the Pacific

After Guadalcanal, the Marines took part in landing after landing, inching their way to victory in the Pacific. At home in the United States, people studied their globes and maps to find out where in the world these strange-sounding places were. Bougainville and Tarawa and Makin were taken. The Japanese commander of Betio, an island targeted in the Tarawa operation, boasted that Betio's air base "could not be taken by one million men in one hundred years." A single division of Marines—about 20,000 men—took the islands in 76 hours.

Then came Kwajalein and Eniwetok. Tinian, Saipan, and Peleliu fell next. After that there was Iwo Jima, described as "the toughest yet," a place where "uncommon valor was

Two Marines use a captured Japanese machine gun to carry on the battle after their own machine gun was disabled on Iwo Jima.

34

common virtue." Finally, there was Okinawa, the last battle.

On Okinawa, as on several earlier island landings, the Marine efforts were helped greatly by Navajo "code talkers." These Native American Marines operated radios between front line units and command posts in the rear. Every important message was sent in the Navajo language. The Japanese never were able to understand the messages.

With the end of the war in 1945, the Marines had come of age, fully. The Corps had an air arm that shot down more than 2,300 enemy planes. It had 19,000 female officers and enlisted women. There were also nearly 20,000 black men and other minorities in the ranks. In the eyes of the world, the United States Marine Corps had earned its title as an elite force, perhaps the finest ever.

Between Wars

Predictably, at the end of the war, the military services saw their numbers shrink. Within two years, the size of the Marine Corps dropped from a wartime high of 485,000 to 92,000. For the next few years, the Corps picked up its continuing battle to survive. The familiar questions arose once again. Should the Marine Corps become part of the Army? Should the Marine Corps be disbanded?

These were also the years when the armed services were unified under a single head. Now all the services would fall under the secretary of defense, a cabinet-level post appointed by the president. The Army Air Corps became a separate service—the Air Force.

Fortunately for the Marine Corps, its long fight for survival was over. Public Law 416, enacted in 1952, guaranteed a

Marine Corps. In the words of the commandant at the time, the new law stated "that the Marine Corps shall be maintained as a ready fighting force prepared to move promptly in time of peace or war to areas of trouble."

Into Korea

While this fight for Marine Corps survival was going on, the Marines were called on once again to go to war. This time it was in Korea.

World War II left the United States as the only real military power in the Pacific. So when North Korean soldiers

With bombing support from its air unit, a division of Marines moves in to attack an enemy roadblock in North Korea. After the Marines successfully invaded North Korea, communist leaders of China, located north and west of North Korea, felt threatened and sent troops to join the fight.

invaded South Korea in 1950, the Marines were soon back in action.

The war lasted three years. It ended without a clear victory for either side. The North Koreans had failed in their attempt to take over South Korea. The United Nations troops, which included the U.S. Marines, signed a cease-fire agreement. The agreement left the two countries virtually as they were before the war began.

Restoring Order

Hardly had the Korean War ended when the Marines were called on yet again. First, they went to Lebanon in 1958. That country's president asked for help in restoring order to his riot-torn land. The outcome was expressed in words the Corps had used time and again: "The Marines have landed and the situation is well in hand."

Two years later, Marines were sent to the Dominican Republic. The country's dictator had been murdered. The Marine Corps again was expected to restore order. Soon after that, the first Marines landed in Vietnam.

The Impossible War

The Marines went into Vietnam in 1965. They stayed for almost a decade. When they finally left, without a victory, most people agreed they had been given an impossible task. Their job was to help put down a revolution by communist citizens of South Vietnam—the Viet Cong—and turn back an invasion by North Vietnamese troops. At the same time, the U.S. government was unwilling to deploy its full military

Two Marines make their way to the top of a hill near a landing beach in Vietnam.

power. After the United States had fought in the war for four years, it began to reduce the numbers of troops sent to fight. Many people in the United States protested U.S. involvement in the war. As the Continental Marines had shown the British 200 years earlier, putting down a revolution thousands of miles from home is not easily done.

The Middle East

The United States has closely watched events in the Middle East and has, at times, sent troops to protect U.S. interests. Marines were aboard Navy ships sent to the Persian Gulf in the late 1980s during the Iran-Iraq War. Then, in 1990, Marine combat troops were among the United Nations forces sent to Saudi Arabia in an effort to persuade Iraqi troops to leave Kuwait. When fighting broke out against Iraq in mid-January of 1991, allied air and ground forces included more than 80,000 Marines.

Present and Future

The Marine Corps is now preparing to enter the 21st century with a strong, up-to-date fighting force. The modern Corps will always be ready to respond when world peace is challenged, to assist worldwide humanitarian efforts, and to help war-torn countries rebuild. The Marines participate in numerous training exercises each year, all over the world, to make sure they will be ready. As long as they stay ready, Marines believe, they will continue to live up to the slogan they earned in World War I: "First to Fight."

The United States sent tens of thousands of Marines to Saudi Arabia to begin a United Nations fight against Iraqi forces that had invaded Kuwait.

40

3
The Once and Future Corps

The modern-day Marine Corps is not at all like the original Continental Marines. But that is to be expected. The world has seen great changes since 1775.

These changes include the discovery and invention of many things industrialized nations now take for granted. Among these are steamships, railroads, automobiles, and airplanes. Modern medicine. Computers. Atomic energy. The list goes on.

Many of these discoveries and inventions made the world seem a smaller place. During the Revolutionary War, a unit of Marines needed nearly two weeks to march from Boston to New York, a distance of about 200 miles. Marines now can be flown to nearly any place in the world in a matter of hours.

The Marine Corps is a force in readiness, prepared to go anywhere within hours of receiving the order, "Move out!"

Marines and the Navy

The Marine Corps, like the Army, Air Force, and Navy, is a separate armed service. At the same time, the Marine Corps is also part of the Department of the Navy, just as the Navy itself is. This means the Marine Corps and the Navy are closely interwoven. For example, Marines go into battle on Navy ships. Amphibious landings are jointly planned and run by Navy and Marine officers.

Marines also serve as part of the crew on certain Navy ships. They guard most naval shore bases at home and abroad. The Navy provides doctors, dentists, nurses, and other medical personnel for the Marines. All the Corps's chaplains—priests, ministers, and rabbis—are Navy officers.

Marines have their own aviators, but their airplanes are bought with Navy funds. Many Marine aviation units serve on Navy aircraft carriers. Marine pilots and flight officers also earn their wings at the Navy's flight schools. Even the wings Marine aviators wear are the same as those worn by Navy fliers.

All this means the Navy and Marines work closely together. It does not mean, however, that there is no rivalry between the two services. Indeed, there is. In a way, it often seems as if the Marines are like star football players. They get most of the glory. But they know that success in warfare, as in football, takes teamwork. If it weren't for the support of the other players—the Navy—there would be no victories.

The Fleet Marine Force

The cutting edge of the Marine Corps is the Fleet Marine Force, the FMF. Actually, there are two Fleet Marine Forces. One, called Marine Forces Atlantic (MARFORLANT) is headquartered at Norfolk, Virginia, and the other, Marine Forces Pacific (MARFORPAC), is headquartered at Camp H. M. Smith in Hawaii. In keeping with the Marine Corps mission to be a force in readiness, both FMFs keep part of their forces at sea on Navy ships at all times.

The U.S. Navy and Marine Corps are closely linked. These members of a Marine detachment from a Navy battleship spot naval gunfire during a training exercise.

The heart of the FMF is the Marine division. Each division (there are three on active duty) has about 20,000 officers and enlisted Marines. Another 1,000 Naval officers and enlisted sailors serve with each Marine division. Besides infantry, artillery, and tanks, the division includes support groups like engineers, medical units, and motor transport units.

Supporting these combat troops in the air are Marine jet fighter-bombers, helicopters, and observation and transport aircraft from the Marine Air Wings. On land, combat troops of the FMF can be beefed up with more engineers, artillery,

Helicopters from the Marine Air Wings support troops by transporting them from site to site, evacuating wounded Marines, and dropping ammunition and supplies.

medics, and tanks as they are needed. The extra troops are drawn from a group of Marine units called Force Troops.

Supporting the combat troops at sea is, of course, the job of the Navy. Over the years, Navy and Marine officers have worked together to design special ships for amphibious assaults. Among these are fast cargo ships for carrying heavy equipment and transport ships for carrying troops. There are also ships that carry tanks and heavy artillery, and others that carry helicopters and armored assault vehicles.

Central to combat support is an idea called "pre-positioning." This means having a number of cargo ships already loaded with enough supplies to support a large Marine force for up to 30 days. Carrying food, ammunition, heavy equipment, and medical supplies—what Marines call "beans, bullets, and bandages"—these ships are kept at various sites around the world. When Marines were sent from the United States to the Persian Gulf in 1990 as part of Operation Desert Shield, several pre-positioned cargo ships were waiting as the troops landed in transport aircraft. Because of pre-positioning, the Marines were ready to fight long before other infantry units.

Of course, not every job calls for the full might of the FMF. That is why "flexible" is the best word to describe the Fleet Marine Force. The size of a unit can be tailored to fit the size of the job at hand. For example, in 1989 the Marine Corps sent a single rifle company—about 200 Marines—to help in a quick strike into Panama. On the other hand, in Vietnam, a long, drawn-out land war, there were up to 86,000 Marine combat troops and aviators in the country at any one time.

The Navy has special ships and landing craft that carry Marine tanks to wherever they are needed.

45

Marine Aviation

May 22, 1912, marks the birth of Marine aviation. That was the date Lieutenant Alfred A. Cunningham was given orders to report to the Navy's new aviation camp at Annapolis, Maryland. In short order—after only 2 hours and 40 minutes of instruction—Lieutenant Cunningham soloed. That flight made him the first Marine aviator.

For the next few years, Marine aviators flew as part of the Navy. In 1915, Marine aviation units were separated from the Navy. Marine aviators were then directed to operate with Marine ground forces as part of an advanced-base force. (An advanced base is usually an overseas base that is not intended to be used as a permanent installation.)

Marine Corps mechanics work on a World War I plane.

In time, having aviators operate with ground forces led to the primary mission of Marine aviation. The mission is to "support the Fleet Marine Force in landing operations and in support of troop activities in the field...." This means that Marine aviation acts as a kind of aerial artillery and transport service. Marine jet fighter-bombers and helicopter gunships, guided to their targets by radio contact with the ground troops, help destroy enemy obstacles so the infantry can move forward. At the same time, other helicopters and giant transport planes quickly move troops and supplies into and out of battle zones. As a result, there are few aces, or "Top Guns" among Marine aviators. Their job is to support Marine infantry, not to look for enemy planes to shoot down.

Support Services

Not all Marines serve in FMF units. There are tens of thousands of Marines working in a variety of other fields. For instance, both Marine officers and enlisted personnel are part of the crews of major Naval ships, such as aircraft carriers and submarine tenders. These seagoing Marines help provide security and perform any other duties the ship's captain (always a Naval officer) requires.

A select group of enlisted Marines serves as Marine security guards at government embassies all over the world. Although a highly prized assignment, embassy duty is not without its dangers. Several incidents in the Middle East and in Latin America proved this to be true. In each case, the small Marine detachment was forced to defend itself— and the civilian embassy workers—against rioting mobs.

Other Marines work at jobs as varied as keeping payroll

Marines in Selected Reserve service board a helicopter during a weekend of training exercises.

and medical records, recruiting, playing in a Marine band, and running a post office. In short, the operation of an organization as large and complex as the United States Marine Corps is an enormous task. It takes a lot of people with a lot of different skills to keep the Corps running smoothly.

The Marine Reserves

The Marine Corps has four divisions and four air wings, plus the support services. This adds up to nearly 291,000 officers and enlisted Marines, men and women.

Three of the Marine divisions and three of the air wings are on active duty. The fourth division and fourth air wing, along with their support services, are part of the Marine Reserves. They are made up of about 106,500 officers and enlisted men and women.

Many of the Marines are in the Selected Reserve. These Marines train one weekend a month and two weeks each summer. They are paid for the days they train and are promoted on schedule with Marines on active duty. Marines in the Selected Reserve can be called to active duty by the president of the United States. The president did just that, beginning in August 1990, when he called several thousand Marines into active duty for Operation Desert Shield and Operation Desert Storm in the Middle East.

A second group of Marines is in the Inactive Reserve. These Marines are not required to drill on weekends or to attend summer training sessions. Nor are they paid. Marines in the Inactive Reserve can be called to active duty by the U.S. Congress.

Female Marines

The first female Marine was Opha M. Johnson. She enlisted as a reservist on April 12, 1918, during World War I. Soon, 276 other women followed her into the Corps. These women, called "Marinettes," worked at desk jobs. They were clerks, typists, and secretaries. With women doing their desk jobs, many male Marines were freed for combat duty. No sooner had the war ended in November of 1918 than the Marinettes were released from active duty and largely forgotten.

When the United States entered World War II in 1941, the idea of enlisting female Marines was again brought up. At first, the commandant flatly refused to listen to arguments for recruiting women. Finally, however, public opinion won out and the Corps, reluctantly, began to accept women into its ranks. They were the last armed service to do so.

Female recruits receive rifle instruction during basic training.

This time was different from World War I. No longer were the women known as Marinettes. They were called Women Marines. No longer were they assigned only to desk work. In fact, many women worked at highly technical jobs and took on great responsibilities. The highest ranking Marinette in World War I was a sergeant. But in World War II, women became commissioned officers—one earned the rank of colonel.

Before the war ended, Women Marines numbered 1,000 officers and 18,000 enlisted. They were led by Colonel Ruth Streeter, who liked to remind people that her women freed the equivalent of an entire Marine division for combat.

In 1992, the 10,400 female Marines were on equal footing with their male counterparts. Women are part of regular and reserve Marine units. Except for the combat arms, women perform the same duties that men perform.

4
Joining the Marines

So you think you might want to become a Marine? The first thing you must do is find out all you can about the Marines. Reading this book will help, but don't stop here. Look for other books about the Marine Corps in your library. See if you can find some copies of *Leatherneck*, a magazine about Marines written by Marines. The articles in *Leatherneck* paint a true picture of life in the Corps.

Search out people who have served in the Marines. Talk to them about their experiences. If there's a Marine Reserve training unit nearby, arrange to visit it. Talk to as many reservists as you can and watch them train.

Talk with your parents about your goals for the future. Then talk to a Marine recruiter if there is one in the city or town where you live. If there isn't, your school counselor should be able to find out where the nearest recruiting station is located.

Call for an appointment, and be ready to ask questions. You will find the recruiter eager to answer them—and to talk about opportunities offered by the Marine Corps. At the same time, the recruiter will also tell you about the kind of young men and women the Marines are looking to recruit.

Sometime during your first meeting, you will be sure to hear something like this from the recruiter: "We don't want anyone who is looking for the easy way. We want people who like a challenge."

All this might suggest that getting into the Marine Corps

will not be easy, and that is true. First of all, you have to *want* to be a Marine. No one is going to force you to enlist. Next, the Marine Corps is a small service. Only the Coast Guard is smaller. The Army, Navy, and Air Force are three times bigger than the Marines, which has approximately 176,100 men and 8,400 women on active duty.

Also, Marines have long been proud of belonging to an elite branch of the military. The Marine Corps wants only the best recruits, and it will be choosy. Often that means setting standards a bit higher than those of the other services. As recruiters like to say, "If everybody could get in the Marines, it wouldn't be the Marines."

Still, each year the Marine Corps looks to recruit several thousand men and women. The terms of enlistment range from three to six years. The number of years a recruit serves depends on what career field he or she chooses. Those who make the grade will serve in one of a number of fields, including aviation, computers, and the combat arms, which include artillery, infantry, and tanks. Women, however, are not allowed to serve in the combat arms.

Basic Requirements

In order to enlist, a candidate must be between the ages of 17 and 29. He or she must be in good health, and be no less than 4 feet, 10 inches and no taller than 6 feet, 7 inches. (In special cases, height requirements can be waived, or put aside.) Weight must be proportionate to height.

Candidates who are 17 years old must have the consent of both parents before they can enlist. All candidates must be citizens of the United States or registered aliens. Finally, since

New recruits line up for a drill during basic training at the Marine Corps Recruit Depot at Parris Island in South Carolina.

the Marine Corps is looking for intelligent, alert recruits, candidates must be high school graduates. These are the basic requirements for enlisting. Although they sound simple enough, they do not tell the whole story.

What might prevent an otherwise qualified candidate from joining the Marines? For one, good health means more than being in top physical condition, free from diseases like asthma or epilepsy. It means moral and mental fitness as well. Any history of drug use or a criminal record is enough to make the Corps turn a candidate away. If the candidate has dependents other than a spouse—a child or a parent to support—he or she will be turned down. New Marines can't be expected to support a family on a private's base pay.

Then there is a series of tests called the Armed Services Vocational Aptitude Battery, or the ASVAB. The tests, which take two and a half hours to complete, measure a whole range of mental and mechanical abilities. For example, they can tell how well a candidate can read, reason, and solve math problems. The test can even indicate if the would-be Marine is better suited to be trained as an electronics repair person, a clerk-typist, or a truck driver.

The other military services—Army, Navy, Air Force, and Coast Guard—will accept a score of 21 (out of a possible 99) as a passing grade. The minimum score for those wanting to become Marines is 31. Two-thirds of all Corps candidates score over 50.

Throughout basic training, Marines will learn the Marine Corps way of doing things, including how to march, stand at attention, and salute.

After boot camp, Marines will train in special areas, such as infantry. *Above*, a Marine learns how to operate an M-47 Dragon anti-tank missile.

Enlistment Programs

Scoring high on the ASVAB tests can be important. Candidates with the highest scores may be accepted into QEP, the Quality Enlistment Program. This program guarantees assignment to one of a number of choice training schools *before* enlistment. Some of the schools bring an immediate promotion to private first class (which means extra pay) and perhaps a cash bonus of several thousand dollars as well.

Against these benefits, the candidate must weigh the fact of a longer term of enlistment. In some programs, such as the high-technology fields of avionics (aviation electronics) or computers, the Marine Corps invests a great deal of time and money in training recruits. In return, each recruit will be asked to serve for four, five, or even six years.

Candidates who wish to enlist before they graduate from high school may do so under DEP, the Delayed Enlistment Program. The candidate enlists, but puts off going on active duty for up to one year. This way, candidates can complete high school and still reserve their place in a career field well in advance.

Enlisting in the Reserves

In addition to the nearly 185,000 Marines on active duty, there are another 106,000 in the Marine Reserves. These are part-time Marines, subject to being called to active duty in times of national emergencies.

Marine reservists live and work (or attend college) as civilians. One weekend each month they train at a Marine Reserve unit near their home. Two weeks each summer they train at a military base.

Marines in the Reserves collect the same pay and benefits as regular Marines, but only for the days they actually train. A new Marine reservist can expect to earn about $1,300 a year at first. Raises in pay come with promotions and length of service.

The term of enlistment for the Marine Reserves is eight years. A reservist first completes basic training just like a regular Marine. After that, he or she goes to a special training school, or home to on-the-job training with a Reserve unit. After three or four years, the reservist no longer has to train on weekends or during the summer.

Boot Camp

All recruits, regulars as well as those in the Reserves, will undergo basic training—or boot camp—either at Parris Island, South Carolina, or in San Diego, California. All female recruits train at Parris Island.

Marine boot camp is tough. It is longer—11 weeks—than basic training in any of the other services. Physically, it is the toughest because the Marine Corps stresses physical conditioning and exercise more than the other services do. Boot camp tests mental skills as well. In short, it will demand much of each recruit.

The first few days of boot camp are taken up with what is known as "processing and forming." This means getting a regulation haircut (it takes only 20 seconds!), having dental

Physical training is a large part of boot camp for recruits, who will test their limits during 16-hour days for approximately three months.

and physical exams, receiving uniforms, and learning about government insurance programs.

During these days, recruits are formed into training platoons of 70 people. Recruits are soon taught the basics of standing at attention, saluting, and marching in close order drill. They are also taught the Marine Corps way to brush teeth, shower, make a bed—even the Marine Corps way to eat!

Recruits quickly learn that tobacco, chewing gum, candy, ice cream, soda pop, and alcohol of any kind are forbidden. They also learn what it feels like to rise every morning at 0530 (5:30 A.M.), or even earlier, and put in week after week of nonstop, 16-hour days that end with taps, or lights out, at 2130 hours (9:30 P.M.). Along the way, recruits learn a whole new vocabulary, one in which floors are "decks," walls are "bulkheads," and windows are "ports."

But most important, this is the time when recruits meet their DIs, or drill instructors. Three or four of them are assigned to each training platoon. All are experienced Marine sergeants who have been carefully picked, and who have completed a school for DIs, which is far tougher than boot camp.

Each DI is a combination of teacher, parent, counselor, and judge. They are firm but fair, demanding but understanding. They do everything they can to make certain recruits succeed. At the same time, DIs tell recruits what is expected from them. What the DIs expect of recruits is contained in the Drill Instructor's Covenant. It reads in part:

- You will treat all Marines with courtesy and respect.
- You must be completely honest in everything you do. A Marine never lies, cheats, or compromises.
- You must respect the rights and property of all other persons. A Marine never steals.

Recruits, *above*, in service uniforms, stand at attention for inspection. Throughout basic training, the recruits are led through drills and inspections by a drill instructor, *left*, who works hard to turn each recruit into a Marine.

- You must be proud of yourself and the uniform you wear.
- You must try your best to learn the things you are taught. Everything we teach you is important and must be remembered.
- You must work hard to strengthen your body.
- Above all else, you must never quit or give up. We cannot train you and help you unless you are willing to give your very best.

Once the business of processing and forming is over, boot camp begins in earnest. For the next 11 weeks, recruits face

Drill instructors hand out graduation certificates to members of the Marine honor guard during ceremonies at the end of basic training.

a hectic schedule of classes, tests, inspections, and physical training.

Classroom subjects include the history of the Marine Corps, first aid, how to wear the uniform, and the code of conduct. Physical training includes daily one-mile runs (building up to five miles), sit-ups, pull-ups, push-ups, and stretching exercises. There are obstacle courses, helicopter and amphibious tank training, exercise and teamwork drills, and survival swim training.

Recruits will learn about the M16A2 rifle—how to march with it, care for it, and shoot it accurately. There are hours of drill in squad tactics and hand-to-hand combat.

Every step of the way, recruits march in close-order drill. They are inspected, taught, tested, and retaught and retested by their DIs. Then, 11 weeks later, after one final five-mile endurance run and one final inspection—this time by top officers at the recruit depot—there is a graduation parade. Recruits wear dress uniforms for the first time. They are filled with a sense of discipline, pride, and self-confidence to a degree they never thought possible.

At the end of graduation day, recruits are finally called by the title they have worked so hard to attain: Marine.

5
Life after Boot Camp

One thing every new Marine quickly learns is that the Marine Corps believes in education. There are more than 500 schools that Marines can attend. Of these, 200 are open to enlisted Marines.

Enlisted Marines can get formal training in courses that are as short as 2 weeks (basic typing or transportation management) or as long as 47 to 50 weeks (foreign language or Hawk missile repair).

Marines continue their schooling once they join a unit. They will be involved constantly in on-the-job training for their occupational fields. Would-be recruits who think experience in the Marines will be a welcome relief from school should think again. Marines are always learning, always going to school.

Choosing an Occupational Field

Marine recruits in the Quality Enlistment Program (QEP) have already been guaranteed their choice for an occupational field before enlisting. They might prefer infantry, printing, or military police. These recruits will not only be guaranteed a slot in the field of their choice, but they will also be able to train for the specialty they want within that field.

Infantry, for example, includes riflemen, machine gunners, mortarmen, and antitank assaultmen. Printing includes basic offset printing and printing equipment repair. QEP recruits who opt for the military police can choose criminal investigation, law enforcement, brig (or jail) guard.

Other Marine recruits will sit down with a Marine counselor after boot camp to determine the occupational field in which they will train. They will be given tests. They will be asked which field, of the 34 open to them, they prefer. Whether recruits get their first choice depends largely on their test scores and on the needs of the Marine Corps.

Some of these Marines may want to become tank crewmen or airborne radio operators. If they qualify, every effort will be made to accommodate them. However, should the Corps need AAV crewmen or air traffic controllers, the new recruits may well end up in one of these specialties.

School of Infantry

Before any training in an occupational field takes place, all male boot camp graduates must first go through four weeks of SOI, the School of Infantry.

All male Marines, officers and enlisted alike, whatever their specialties, are considered riflemen first. There is a story, often told, of a Marine jet pilot being interviewed by a newspaper reporter. The pilot was asked what his job was in the Marine Corps. "Well," he answered, "I am a Marine rifleman on temporary duty as a jet pilot."

All Marines qualify—that is, shoot for scores—with their rifle every year. In addition, sometime during each year, those Marines who normally work in jobs such as truck driving, supply clerking, or computer programming will most likely get some kind of infantry training.

SOI takes up where boot camp left off. There is more

At the School of Infantry, Marines receive advanced combat and weaponry training. *Above,* **a camouflaged Marine points out a target for a sniper.**

training with weapons, including rifles, 9-millimeter pistols, machine guns, grenade launchers, and mortars. There are classes and field training exercises in camouflage and concealment, in digging a fighting hole, and in squad and platoon movements.

The training takes place during the day and at night, in good weather and in bad. Throughout, there are mock battles and long marches across unmarked terrain with only a map and a compass for guides. And there are parades, inspections, testing, and retesting. Once SOI is over, each graduate has a much better idea of what being a Marine is all about.

Duty Stations

The Marine Corps maintains several large bases and many smaller installations in the United States. The first base seen by all enlisted recruits is the recruit depot. One is at Parris Island in South Carolina. The other is at San Diego, California. (Recruits in officer training programs are sent to Quantico, Virginia.)

Recruits who take boot camp at Parris Island will go on to Camp Lejeune in North Carolina for SOI. Camp Lejeune is part of MARFORLANT and also the home of the Second Marine Division. Near Camp Lejeune, at Cherry Point and

Marines can be shipped to stations across the world. These Marines are participating in an exercise on the Philippine Islands.

at New River, are Marine Corps air stations. These house the Second Marine Air Wing.

Recruits who attend boot camp in San Diego will go on to nearby Camp Pendleton for SOI. Camp Pendleton is also the home of the First Marine Division. A few miles north of Camp Pendleton are Marine Corps air stations at El Torro and at Tustin. These are the homes of the Third Marine Air Wing. Hawaii's Camp Smith serves as headquarters for MARFORPAC.

In addition to these, the Marine Corps has a large supply depot, a mountain warfare school, and artillery ranges in California. Another supply base is located in Georgia. There are also air stations in Arizona and South Carolina.

The Marine Corps Development and Education Command is in Quantico, Virginia. Headquarters for the entire Corps is located a few miles north of Quantico, in Washington, D.C.

Overseas, Marines can be found in varying numbers at virtually every Naval base. The Corps operates its own bases in Japan (part of the First Marine Air Wing) and on Okinawa (home of the Third Marine Division and the rest of the First Marine Air Wing).

Special Duty

A number of duty stations aside from the FMF are open to selected Marines in most occupational fields. Sea duty (for men) and embassy duty are only two of these.

Every shore base has troops on barracks duty. Camp Pendleton, for example, requires the services of thousands of Marines, from clerks to truck drivers, and from cooks and bakers to military police.

Perhaps the most prized barracks duty of all is at the

Marine Corps Headquarters at Eighth and I streets in Washington, D.C. That is where the commandant lives. Marines stationed there help guard the president of the United States and serve as honor guards on special occasions.

Other Marines are posted to "I and I" duty. This involves working as instructors and inspectors at Marine Reserve training centers. These centers are scattered across the country, from Maine to Florida, from Massachusetts to Oregon, as well as in Hawaii and Alaska.

A very select group of Marines will be picked for recruiting duty. Since they represent the Corps to civilians, recruiters are very carefully chosen. They must be strong communicators and know all there is to know about the Corps.

Finally, there are Marine drill instructors, the DIs. After a rugged, nine-week training course, DIs are sent to one of the recruit depots. Their job, a very important one, is to turn raw recruits into Marines in 11 short weeks.

Marines stationed at the Marine Corps Headquarters help to guard the president of the United States. The president frequently takes short-distance flights in Marine helicopters.

The Marine Band

The Marine Corps maintains several bands. Chief among these is the band known as "The President's Own," the United States Marine Band. It is the official White House and presidential ceremonial band.

The band was founded around 1800 by Commandant William Ward Burrows. Some years later, John Philip Sousa became its leader. Sousa is noted for having written more than 100 marches. One of these, *Semper Fidelis* (meaning "Always Faithful," which is the Marine motto), is the official march of the Corps.

Musicians are enlisted directly from civilian life for duty with the band. Getting into the band is not easy. All prospective members have to display their ability to play several instruments. Members of The President's Own do not go to boot camp and are not expected to be ready for combat.

John Philip Sousa, shown here leading a Navy band during World War I, served as director of the Marine Band from 1880 to 1892. Sousa wrote over 100 marches during that time, and his music is performed all over the world more than a century later.

The Marine Corps has several bands, which perform at various ceremonies.

Besides The President's Own, the Marine Corps has a number of other bands and drum and bugle units. Men and women who qualify (they must pass a musical audition) will first go to boot camp and SOI. After that, they're off to the Marine Corps School of Music or the Drum and Bugle School. Both schools, held in Little Creek, Virginia, last 24 weeks. From there graduates join Marine Corps field bands or drum and bugle units in the FMF or at major bases.

Pay and Benefits

When the first Continental Marines signed up in November 1775, they were promised $10 a month for their services. Like the Minutemen who fought at Lexington and Concord seven months earlier, these new Marines carried their own muskets.

Before the Revolutionary War ended in 1781, those same Marines were clothed in green uniforms with white trim and were armed with government muskets. They were fed (most of the time) and paid (some of the time). Without a doubt, these first Marines did not enlist for the chance to become rich.

Nor have Marines since then enlisted primarily for the money. A private in World War II, for example, was paid $50 a month. As late as the Korean War in the 1950s, privates were paid $75 a month, and second lieutenants were paid less than $5,000 a year.

In recent years, however, the pay, allowances, and benefits for Marines have improved greatly. From the first day the recruits take the oath of enlistment, their base pay is just under $700 a month. After boot camp, they will get a raise to well above $700. From then on, pay raises are tied into promotions and time in service. Should a recruit make sergeant within four years, he or she can expect a base pay of well over $1,000 a month. Sergeant majors, the top enlisted grade, can expect to earn nearly $3,000 a month in base pay at the peak of their careers.

Base pay is only one part of the benefits. Newly enlisted recruits who qualify can get bonuses. Depending on the length of enlistment, the occupational field, and test scores, these bonuses can reach as much as $7,000. Marines who reenlist can earn additional bonuses equal to as much as five years of pay.

Every enlisted Marine is given free medical and dental care, housing, and meals. There is extra money—and medical and dental care—for dependents. Marines who are not housed at a military base will get extra money to help pay the rent. There are savings and insurance programs as well. And every Marine is given 30 days of paid vacation each year. Officers get most of these same benefits, except they pay for their uniforms (after an initial clothing allowance of $300) and meals.

Marines can shop at the post's commissary (supermarket) and exchange (department store). These stores generally offer special bargains on items that range from breakfast cereals to compact disc players.

Finally, for career Marines, there is a retirement program. After 20 years of service, Marines can retire with a yearly pension that amounts to half their base pay. After 30 years, they can receive about 75 percent of their base pay. Retired Marines and their dependents keep their post shopping privileges and medical and dental care.

6
Going for the Gold

Among the 184,500 Marines on active duty are 17,300 commissioned officers. The 10 grades for commissioned officers range in rank from second lieutenant to four-star general. Both the commandant and the assistant commandant of the Marine Corps are four-star generals.

Included among the 17,300 commissioned officers are 550 women. The highest ranking female officer is a one-star, or brigadier, general. Newly commissioned officers must go through a 21-week basic school before they train in an occupational field.

In addition to commissioned officers, the Marine Corps has 1,830 warrant officers. All warrant officers are appointed directly from the ranks of enlisted Marines.

Before any enlisted Marine can be considered for appointment as a warrant officer, he or she will have many years of experience in a special field such as personnel, computers, or ordnance (ammunition and weapons). The four grades of warrant officer, from W-1 to W-4, correspond in rank to second lieutenant, first lieutenant, captain, and major among commissioned officers.

Where Marine Officers Come From

For the first hundred years of its life, the Marine Corps did not have any formal programs to select or train its officers. In those years, some officers were commissioned directly from civilian life. Others quit the military service academies—the Army's at West Point, New York, or the Navy's at Annapolis, Maryland—to take commissions. Still others were chosen by the commandant. Because there were no fixed standards, not all Marine officers were qualified to hold their positions.

This began to change in 1882. That was the year Congress told the commandant that at least some of his officers had to be graduates of the Naval Academy. Before long *every* Marine officer was an Annapolis graduate.

As the Corps began to grow, however, it became apparent that there had to be other sources from which to choose

During Officer Candidates Class, physical training is a part of the daily activities.

officers. In recent times, only between 10 and 15 percent of the graduates of the Naval Academy have been offered commissions as second lieutenants in the Marine Corps.

Over the years, other programs for turning out Marine officers were developed. Several of these programs are still in existence. Among them are NROTC (Naval Reserve Officers Training Corps), PLC (Platoon Leaders Class), and OCC (Officer Candidates Class). The newest program is WOCP, (Women Officer Candidates Program).

In addition to these, there are two special officer candidate programs. One is for those who wish to become Marine aviators. The other is for those who wish to become Marine lawyers.

Very few of the officer candidates in these programs have had any military experience. Yet they all have one thing in common. Every officer candidate is a college graduate, or is enrolled in college and expects to graduate. The Marine Corps believes college is the first training ground for would-be officers.

The U.S. Naval Academy

When the first graduates of the Naval Academy accepted commissions as Marine second lieutenants in 1882, the Academy was nearly 40 years old. It has since grown into an internationally recognized four-year college with approximately 4,300 students.

The Naval Academy accepts about 1,300 new students each year. Ten percent of these are women. Entering students, or plebes, as they are called, are high school graduates between the ages of 17 and 22. They are U.S. citizens, physically

Some Marine Corps officers are graduates of the U.S. Naval Academy in Annapolis, Maryland. They receive commissions as second lieutenants upon graduation.

healthy and of good moral character. All are unmarried and have no dependents.

Getting into the Naval Academy is not easy. There are far more candidates than there are openings. As a result, only the best make the grade. The first step is to get nominated, usually by a member of Congress. (Candidates can write to their legislators and ask to be considered for a nomination.) After receiving a nomination, a candidate must pass a tough physical examination and an even tougher series of physical fitness tests.

Top grades in high school are important, of course. But the admitting officers will look at the nominee's complete record. Has he or she been active in clubs and athletics? What about community service? Jobs? Scouting? The Naval Academy is interested in turning out leaders. That's why they want well-rounded plebes, not just computer whizzes, bookworms, or athletes.

Those who are accepted will be paid from the start. More-over, tuition, books, meals, uniforms, and medical and dental care are free. The candidate's four years are spent studying subjects like engineering, English, history, math, and science. In addition there will be classes in maritime subjects like navigation and gunnery.

Despite a demanding academic schedule, there will be time for other activities. These range from athletics (required of everyone) to drama club, and from drum and bugle corps to sailing. Summers are spent at sea on Navy ships or aircraft, or at a major naval base.

Graduates of the Naval Academy are awarded bachelor's degrees and commissions as ensigns in the Navy, or, for a select few, as second lieutenants in the Marine Corps. These new officers are required to spend a minimum of five years on active duty, and their starting base pay is about $1,400 a month.

Naval Academy Preparatory School

Candidates who do not make it into the Naval Academy have another choice. They can be admitted after spending a year at the Naval Academy Preparatory School in Newport, Rhode Island. Most students at NAPS, as it is known, lack a few credits in key subjects such as English, math, or science. NAPS gives students the chance to earn those credits.

NAPS is also a way for high school graduates who do not try for a nomination to enter the Naval Academy. These candidates first enlist in the Reserves, then attend the prep school. Ordinarily, every one of the candidates who completes the prep school year will be given an appointment to the Naval Academy. If, for some reason, a prep school graduate is not admitted, he or she can return to civilian life.

NROTC programs give future Navy and Marine Corps officers an opportunity to earn college diplomas, attending classes like any other college student.

Naval Reserve Officers Training Corps (NROTC)

In many ways, getting accepted into the NROTC programs offered at many colleges is as tough as getting an appointment to the Naval Academy. For one, competition for openings is just as fierce. The academic and physical requirements are just as strict.

Those who are accepted can attend any of 66 colleges and universities that have NROTC programs. Tuition, books, fees, room and board, and all uniforms are provided free. What is more, NROTC students are paid $100 a month while attending school.

NROTC students who intend to become Marine officers are placed in the Marine option program. Summer training for men includes a 6-week cruise at sea the first year and a 4-week course in warfare the second year. Students attend a 6-week (10-week for women) summer training program with the Marines after their junior year. NROTC graduates are commissioned as second lieutenants and must serve a minimum of four years on active duty.

Those students who apply, but are not selected, for the NROTC scholarship program have another choice. They can participate in a program for students already in college. This program does not pay tuition or other expenses, but it provides $100 a month to selectees during their junior and senior years. Sometime before they graduate, these students will spend a summer training session with the Marines. Like other NROTC graduates, these students are commissioned as second lieutenants in the Marine Corps and serve a minimum of four years on active duty.

Platoon Leaders Class (PLC)

Platoon Leaders Class is a boot camp for would-be Marine officers who are attending college. Male students who join the PLC during their freshman or sophomore year are paid while spending two six-week training sessions at the Marine Corps base in Quantico, Virginia.

Male or female students who join the PLC program in their junior year will spend one 10-week training session at Quantico. All training takes place in the summer, so there will be no interruption of schooling. When the students graduate, they will receive commissions as second lieutenants and will serve a minimum of four years on active duty.

Officer Candidates Class (OCC)

Officer Candidates Class is open to young men who are college seniors or college graduates. In this program, the candidate goes through one 10-week program similar to that given to PLCs. Like PLC graduates, the OCC graduate is commissioned as a second lieutenant after graduation and will serve at least four years on active duty.

Women Officer Candidates Program (WOCP)

The Women Officer Candidates Program is open to women who are in their junior or senior year of college, or who

A platoon of women in the Women Officer Candidates Program march in close-order drill at the Marine Corps Development and Education Command in Quantico, Virginia.

Combat training is part of officer training. Here, a sergeant demonstrates an exercise for a platoon of officer candidates.

are college graduates. Each female candidate must complete a single 10-week summer training session at Quantico.

Except for jobs that might put them into combat—such as machine gunner or assault crewman—female commissioned officers can serve in any field open to male officers.

Special Officer Candidate Programs

The PLC program offers two special options for candidates. PLC-Aviation is for those men who wish to become Marine pilots or flight officers. The program offers a chance for the candidate to get free civilian flight instruction while still in college. Once the PLC-Aviation candidates finish flight training (which usually takes anywhere from 8 to 16 months) and earn their wings, they must serve an additional

Marines who want to fly for the Marine Corps can enroll in the PLC-Aviation program.

five years on active duty. Since the Marine Corps has no female pilots or flight officers, PLC-Aviation is open to men only.

PLC-Law is open to both men and women. In this program, candidates don't go on active duty until they get their law degree and pass the state bar exam that allows them to practice law. Meanwhile, they are commissioned after graduating from college and are promoted on schedule. PLC-Law candidates are likely to be first lieutenants by the time they go on active duty.

From Enlisted Marine to Commissioned Officer

A great number of Marine officers are college graduates who were new to military life when they earned their commissions. At the same time, the Corps has always offered enlisted men and women the chance to become officers.

In times of war, for example, numbers of outstanding enlisted Marines have been awarded commissions as the need arose. There are several paths to a commission for enlisted Marines.

One program allows enlisted Marines, whether regular or reserve, to enter the Naval Academy Preparatory School and then go on to the Naval Academy. Each year, NAPS accepts up to 170 Navy and Marine enlisted men and women into this program.

A second program is known as MECEP—the Marine Enlisted Commissioning Education Program. This is open to outstanding enlisted Marines, no matter what military job they hold. Those who are chosen will be sent to college for up to four years at the expense of the Marine Corps. Once they graduate and complete Officer Candidates Class, the Marines are commissioned as second lieutenants.

Finally, a limited number of warrant officers are picked to be commissioned as LDOs—limited duty officers. Those who are chosen receive commissions as first lieutenants.

Conclusion

Surely not everyone is suited to be a Marine. That is something each person thinking about joining the Marines has to decide.

If you are thinking about enlisting, there are a few points you should keep in mind. One is that the Marine slogan, "First to Fight," is no idle boast. Forty-eight streamers fly from the Marine Corps flag. Each one represents a major battle. In addition, Marines have been rushed hundreds of times to trouble spots all over the world when called upon by the president. Their job in modern times, as it was 200 years ago, is to protect the lives, property, and interests of United States citizens.

You should understand, too, that service in the Marine Corps is not a "9-to-5" job. It is a way of life. In effect, Marines are always on call, always on duty.

Finally, Marine computer operators, truck drivers, aviators, musicians, cooks, and bakers—whatever the job—will have less freedom and quite likely earn less money than their civilian counterparts. But the Marine Corps offers something no other way of life can. That is a sense of *esprit de corps*, which can be summed up in these words: A Marine will never let another Marine down, no matter what the place, no matter what the circumstances. On the ball field and the battlefield, Marines stick together.

For those who qualify, life in the Marine Corps will result in experiences and memories they will carry all their lives. This is as true for those who serve for 3 years as for those who serve for 30. As more than one veteran has noted, "There are no ex-Marines, there are only former Marines."

Appendix

In the United States Marine Corps, officers and enlisted personnel hold different ranks, each with its own pay grade. List A shows the ranks for enlisted personnel (those who sign up with a recruiter) in order from lowest to highest. List B shows the ranks for warrant officers (who are appointed from the ranks of the enlisted). List C shows the ranks for the commissioned officers (who are commissioned from NROTC programs, the Naval Academy, or who are given special officer training by the Marine Corps).

List A
Private First Class
Lance Corporal
Corporal
Sergeant
Staff Sergeant
Gunnery Sergeant
Master Sergeant
First Sergeant
Master Gunnery Sergeant
Sergeant Major
Sergeant Major of the Marine
  Corps

List B
Warrant Officer
Chief Warrant Officer-2
Chief Warrant Officer-3
Chief Warrant Officer-4

List C
Second Lieutenant
First Lieutenant
Captain
Major
Lieutenant Colonel
Colonel
Brigadier General
Major General
Lieutenant General
General

Index

American Revolution.
See Revolutionary
War
amphibious assaults,
7-8, 13, 31, 33-35, 42
Armed Services
Vocational Aptitude
Battery (ASVAB),
54-55
Arnold, Benedict, 14
aviation (in Marine
Corps), 29, 35, 43,
46-47

Barbary states, 16
Barnett, George, 26
barracks duty, 67-68
basic training, 53, 54,
56, 57-61. *See also*
boot camp
Belleau Wood, battle
of, 26-29
benefits, for enlisted
Marines, 71-72
Bonhomme Richard,
the, 13, 14
boot camp, 9, 57-61
Burrows, William
Ward, 69

Camp Lejeune, 10, 66
Camp Pendleton, 67
Chapultepec, Battle
of, 20-21
Civil War, 18, 22
commissioned
officers, 73-83
Concord, Battle of, 11

Confederate Marines,
22
Constitution, the, 15,
17
Continental Marines,
11-14, 38, 41, 70-71
Continental Navy, 14
Cunningham, Alfred
A., 46

Declaration of
Independence, 11
Delayed Enlistment
Program (DEP), 56
Dragon anti-tank
missile, 55
drill instructors, 58-60,
61, 68
Drum and Bugle
School, 70

enlistment, 51-56
esprit de corps, 10, 84
expansionism, 19,
21-22

Fillmore, Millard, 21, 22
Fleet Marine Force,
10, 42-43, 45, 47

Guadalcanal, Battle of,
33, 34
Guerriere, the, 17

Harrier jets, 7
Henderson, Archibald,
19-20

Iran, 38
Iraq, 38-39
Iwo Jima, amphibious
assault on, 34-35

Jackson, Andrew, 18
Johnson, Opha M., 49
Jones, John Paul, 14

Korean War, 36-37
Kuwait, 39

Leatherneck
(magazine), 51
"leatherneck," origin
of, 31
Lexington, Battle of, 11

M16A2 rifle, 61
Maine, the, 23
Marine Corps
Developmental
and Education
Command, 67, 80
Marine Corps Head-
quarters (Eighth
and I), 68
Marine Enlisted
Commissioning
Education Program
(MECEP), 83
Marine Reserves, 48-
49, 51, 56, 57, 68
Marinettes, 49, 50
Mexican War, 20-21
Midway, Battle of, 33
Montezuma, halls of, 20

Navajo code talkers, 35
Naval Academy, the, 74-77, 83
Naval Academy Preparatory School (NAPS), 77, 83
Naval Reserve Officers Training (NROTC), 75, 78-79
Navy, Department of, 41
Navy frogmen, 8
Navy-Marine Corps relationship, 41, 43-45
New Orleans, Battle of, 18
Nicholas, Samuel B., 11, 12-13

O'Bannon, Presley, 16, 25
occupational fields, 63-70
Officer Candidates Class (OCC), 74, 75, 80, 83
officer training, 66, 73-83
Okinawa, 35, 67
"Old Ironsides." See Constitution, the
Operation Desert Shield, 45, 49
Operation Desert Storm, 49

Pearl Harbor, attack on, 31-33
Perry, Matthew Calbraith, 21-22

Pershing, John J., 27
Persian Gulf, 38, 45
pirates, 16, 17
Platoon Leaders Class (PLC), 75, 79-80, 81-82
"President's Own, The." See United States Marine Band

Quality Enlistment Program (QEP), 55-56, 63, 64

recruit depots, 66
retirement (from Marines), 72
Revolutionary War, 11-14, 18, 25, 41, 70

salary (for Marines), 71
Saudi Arabia, 39
School of Infantry, 9-10, 64-66
School of Music, 70
Sea Stallion helicopter, 7
Second Continental Congress, 11, 12
Semper Fidelis, 69
Serapis, the, 13, 14
Sousa, John Philip, 69
Spanish-American War, 23, 29
Streeter, Ruth, 50

United Nations forces, 37, 38
United States Marine Band, 69-70

Vietnam War, 37-38

War of 1812, 17, 18
warrant officers, 73, 83
Washington, George, 14
West Point, 74
Women Marines, 50
Women Officer Candidates Program (WOCP), 75, 80-81
World War I, 25-29, 31, 49, 50
World War II, 31-35, 49, 50. 71

Photo Credits

The photographs in this book are reproduced courtesy of: pp. 1, 6 (by Sgt. C. Archuleta), 50, 53 (by Sgt. Flowers), 54 (by Sgt. A.D. Gruart), 55, 57, 59 top, 60, 62, 65 (by Cpl. Kenneth M. Dvorak), 68 (by Sgt. A.D. Gruart), 74 (by Sgt. G.T. Shingu), 80 (by Sgt. G.T. Shingu), 81 (by Sgt. G.T. Shingu), 82, Department of Marine Corps; pp. 2 (by JO1 Kip Burke), 8 (by PHC Ed Bailey), 9 (by PH2 Eddie C. Cordero), 13 (by PH3 N.C. Barrett from oil painting by William Elliott), 16, 17 (from oil painting by Birch), 39 (by PH2 Thomas Witham), 40 (by PH2 Paul T. Erickson), 43 (by PH1 Jeff Hilton), 44 (by PHC Chet King), 45 (by PHC Ed Bailey), 48 (by PH2 Sean K. Doyle), 59 (by JO1 Jim Bryant), 66 (by PH2 Eddie C. Cordero), 70 (by PH3 Kenneth V. Flemings), Department of Navy; pp. 11, 12, 16, 19, 20, 21, 23, 26 (from painting by Louis H. Gebhardt), 27, 28, 30 top (by George W. Kass), 30 bottom, 35 (by Sgt. J.T. Dreyfuss), 37 (by Cpl. McDonald), 38 (by W.F. Dickman), 46, 69, National Archives; pp. 15, 24, Library of Congress; p. 32, U.S. Army; p. 76, U.S. Naval Academy/K.J. Mierzejewski; and p. 78, University of Minnesota NROTC.

Cover photographs are courtesy of the United States Marine Corps. Front cover photograph by Vincent E. Aldridge.